TAKE-OFF!

The Life and Work of

Wassily Kandinsky

Paul Flux

Heinemann
LIBRARY

www.heinemann.co.uk/library

Visit our website to find out more information about Heinemann Library books.

To order:

 Phone 44 (0) 1865 888066

 Send a fax to 44 (0) 1865 314091

 Visit the Heinemann Bookshop at www.heinemann.co.uk/library to browse our catalogue
and order online.

First published in Great Britain by Heinemann Library, Halley Court, Jordan Hill, Oxford OX2 8EJ,
a division of Reed Educational and Professional Publishing Ltd. Heinemann is a registered trademark
of Reed Educational and Professional Publishing Ltd.

OXFORD MELBOURNE AUCKLAND JOHANNESBURG BLANTYRE
GABORONE IBADAN PORTSMOUTH (NH) USA CHICAGO

© Reed Educational and Professional Publishing Ltd 2002
The moral right of the proprietor has been asserted.

Designed by Celia Floyd
Illustrations by Sam Thompson
Originated by Dot Gradations Ltd
Printed and bound in by South China Printing in Hong Kong/China

ISBN 0 431 13161 9 (hardback)   ISBN 0 431 13166 X (paperback)
06 05 04 03 02   06 05 04 03 02
10 9 8 7 6 5 4 3 2 1   10 9 8 7 6 5 4 3 2 1

British Library Cataloguing in Publication Data

Flux, Paul
  The life and work of Wassily Kandinsky
  1. Kandinsky, Wassily, 1866–1944
  2. Painters – Russia (Federation) – Biography – Juvenile literature
  3. Painting – Russia (Federation) – Juvenile literature
  I. Title II. Wassily Kandinsky
  759.7

Acknowledgements

The publishers would like to thank the following for permission to reproduce photographs: © ADAGP, Paris DACS, London 2002. AKG: p20, Buhrle
Collection, Zurich p11, Lenbachlaus, Munich p21; Bridgeman Art Library: p4, Kunstsammlung Nordrhein-Westfalen, Dusseldorf p15, Musée National d'Art
Moderne, Paris p19, Private Collection p13, Roger Viollet p26, Solomon R Guggenheim Museum, New York p17, Tretyakov Gallery, Moscow, Russia p7; ©
Foto: Städtische Galerie im Lenbachhaus: p9; Hulton Archive: pp10, 16; RMN: pp5, 22; The Solomon R Guggenheim Foundation, New York: David Heald
pp23, 25, 27, 29.

Cover photograph: *Composition 4*, 1911, reproduced with permission of The Art Archive/Kunstsammlung Norshein West.

Our thanks to Sue Graves and Hilda Reed for their advice and expertise in the preparation of this book.

Every effort has been made to contact copyright holders of any material reproduced in this book. Any omissions will be rectified in subsequent printings if
notice is given to the publishers.

Contents

Any words appearing in the text in bold, **like this**, are explained in the Glossary.

Who was Wassily Kandinsky?

Wassily Kandinsky was a Russian painter. He is well known for his **abstract** pictures. He was also a teacher who **inspired** many other artists with his ideas.

A photo of Wassily Kandinsky.

Wassily
Kandinsky

4

Kandinsky was one of the first artists to paint abstract shapes in bright colours. His paintings don't always look like something from real life. His pictures show new ways of arranging coloured shapes.

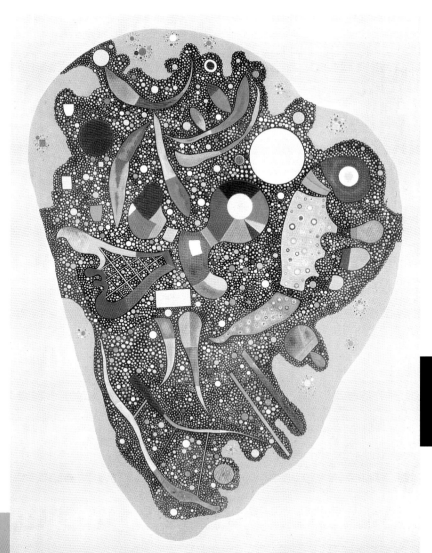

Kandinsky liked to paint free, curving shapes. How many different shapes can you see in this picture?

Colourful Ensemble, 1938

5

Early years

Wassily Kandinsky was born on 4 December 1866, in **Moscow** in Russia. In 1871 his parents **divorced**. Wassily moved to Odessa, also in Russia, to live with his aunt.

Wassily went to live with his aunt.

aunt

Wassily

In 1889 Wassily visited northern Russia. There he saw art made by the local people. He loved what he saw and began to paint pictures of the places he knew.

The Port of Odessa, 1890

Work out how old Kandinsky was when he painted this picture.

Teaching and learning

In 1892, Kandinsky married his cousin, Anya Shemiakina. A year later he began to teach at the University of **Moscow**.

Kandinsky teaching at the University of Moscow.

Wassily

In 1900 Kandinsky began to study art in Munich, in Germany. There he helped start a group of artists called the 'Phalanx'.

Experiments with colour

In 1905 Kandinsky saw a special **exhibition**. All the painters there used strong colours. Henri Matisse was the leader of this group. After this, Kandinsky became **bolder** in his use of colour.

Henri Matisse

canvas

bold colour

Kandinsky liked the bold use of colour in Matisse's paintings.

The Blue Rider, 1903

The rider in this painting is St George, **patron saint** of England. He is riding out to make the world a better place to live in. Kandinsky wanted his paintings to change the world, too.

Read the story about St George. How did he try and make the world a better place to live in?

A fresh start

Kandinsky

Kandinsky travelling on a train.

Kandinsky travelled a lot in France and Russia. In 1908 he moved back to Munich, in Germany. There his paintings became more colourful and less **realistic**.

Kandinsky painted this picture in Murnau, a small town in Germany. He has not tried to show us exactly what he could see. The painting is an **impression** of the view.

Look at this picture and the one on page 7. See how Kandinsky's style of painting has changed.

Road at Murnau, 1909

New ideas

In 1911 Kandinsky helped to organize another **exhibition**. All the artists were trying to find exciting ways to paint.

Kandinsky even experimented with writing poetry.

paintings

poetry

Between 1910 and 1939 Kandinsky painted ten large pictures he called 'Compositions'. Look at this picture and you will see that it is made up of shapes and blocks of colour, rather than real objects.

Composition IV was one of the first **abstract** pictures ever painted.

Painting shapes

In 1911 Kandinsky and his wife were **divorced**. By 1913 Kandinsky had decided to paint only **abstract** shapes. His paintings were shown in New York, USA. People had to look carefully to see what Kandinsky had painted.

skyscrapers

The New York skyline in the early 1900s.

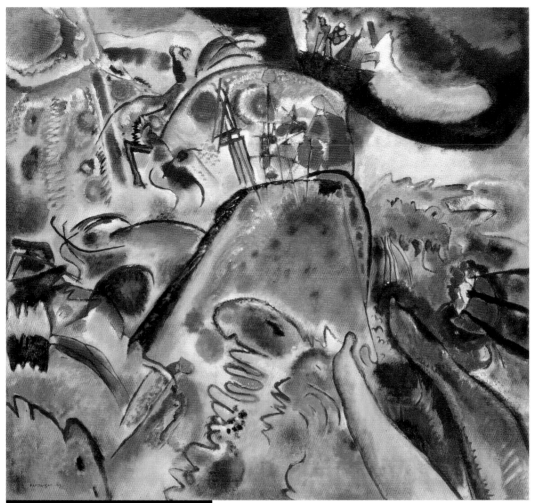

Small Pleasures, 1913

Kandinsky now tried to fill his pictures with shapes and colours. He said that this painting made him think of the sound of small falling drops of water.

Look carefully at this painting. Describe to a friend what this painting makes you think of.

Back to Moscow

After **World War I** began in 1914, Kandinsky returned to **Moscow**. There he met Nina Andreevskaya. They were married in 1917.

Wassily Kandinsky and Nina Andreevskaya.

When the war ended, Kandinsky hoped that his homeland would be a good place to live.

After the war, Kandinsky did paintings that were bright. They showed that he was hopeful of the future.

In Grey, 1919

Teaching art

In December 1921 Kandinsky and his wife left **Moscow** again, to travel to Germany. Kandinsky began teaching at the **Bauhaus**, a famous art school.

Kandinsky was excited about teaching at the Bauhaus.

Bauhaus
art school

Kandinsky stayed at the Bauhaus in Weimar until 1933.

This was one of Kandinsky's last Russian paintings. He was still painting coloured shapes. He often painted circles. He thought these were the most perfect shapes of all.

Red Spot II, 1921

Look carefully at this painting. How many circles can you see? Are they all the same size?

At the Bauhaus

Kandinsky was very busy with his teaching at the **Bauhaus**, but he also painted a lot. Other artists at the school designed furniture.

An artist at the Bauhaus named this chair after Kandinsky.

arms

back

seat

This is one of Kandinsky's most important pictures from this time. The colours, shapes and spaces between them all balance together perfectly. The other artists at the Bauhaus **inspired** Kandinsky to do some of his very best work.

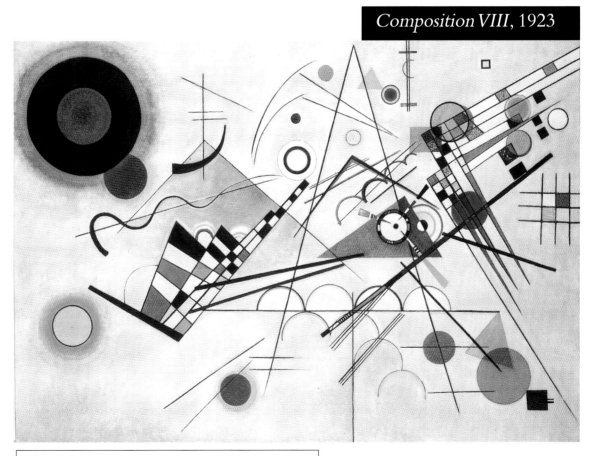

Composition VIII, 1923

How many different colours and shapes can you see in this picture?

The end of the Bauhaus

In 1933 **Adolf Hitler** took power in Germany. He did not like the kind of art the **Bauhaus** was teaching.

German soldiers

The Bauhaus was closed by the German **government**, which was led by Adolf Hitler. The teachers moved to other countries.

German soldiers closing the Bauhaus.

This was one of the last paintings that Kandinsky did in Germany. He knew he would not be safe there any longer.

Decisive Pink, 1932

Living in Paris

In Paris, Kandinsky tried to make money by selling his paintings. These were difficult years for him. An **exhibition** held in 1937 helped more people to see his work.

Kandinsky preparing his paintings for the exhibition.

abstract painting

During the last ten years of his life, Kandinsky used his old ideas about painting, together with the new ideas he used at the Bauhaus.

26

In 1939 war broke out once more. In 1940 German soldiers entered Paris, but Kandinsky stayed in the city. He tried to carry on as normal. He still painted many well-known shapes, like the red circle here.

Around the Circle, 1940

Final days

Kandinsky became ill during the war. He still wanted to find new ways to show his thoughts in his art. He used bright colours and shapes to show what he was feeling.

Kandinsky continued to paint right up to his death.

Kandinsky

canvas

easel

palette

This painting was completed the year before Kandinsky's death and two years before the war ended. Why do you think he used these colours?

Kandinsky died on 13 December 1944. This is one of the last paintings he did. He is remembered for his work on new ways of painting.

Timeline

1866	Wassily Kandinsky is born in **Moscow**, Russia, on 4 December.
1871	Wassily's parents **divorce**. Wassily is brought up by an aunt.
1879	The artist Paul Klee is born.
1886	Kandinsky studies at Moscow University.
1892	He marries his cousin, Anya Shemiakina.
1893	He teaches at Moscow University.
1896	He begins to study art seriously and moves to Munich, in Germany.
1900	He studies at the Munich Academy of Art.
1901	He helps to start the 'Phalanx' group of artists.
1911	Kandinsky and his wife are divorced. He helps put on the first **'Blue Rider' exhibition**.
1914	**World War I** begins. Kandinsky escapes to Switzerland and goes back to Moscow.
1917	Kandinsky marries Nina Andreevskaya. They have a son, Vsevdod.
1920	Vsevdod dies.
1921	Kandinsky and his wife return to Germany.
1922	Kandinsky starts work at the **Bauhaus** art school.
1923	He has one-man show in New York.
1933	The Bauhaus is closed. Kandinsky moves to Paris, France.
1939	**World War II** begins.
1944	Wassily Kandinsky dies in France, aged 78, on 13 December.

Glossary

abstract   art which does not try to show people or things. It uses shape and colour to make the picture.

Adolf Hitler   German leader from 1933 to 1945

Bauhaus   famous art school in Germany

Blue Rider   group of artists in Germany, started in 1911, led by Wassily Kandinsky and Franz Marc

bolder   braver

divorce   end a marriage

exhibition   art on display for people to see

experiment   try things out

government   group of people who rule a country

impression   sense of what is there

inspire   get good ideas from someone else

Moscow   capital city of Russia

patron saint   holy person who watches over a country

realistic   trying to show something as it really is

World War I   war in Europe that lasted from 1914 to 1918

World War II   war involving many important nations fought in Europe, Africa and Asia from 1939 to 1945

More books to read

How Artists Use Shape, Paul Flux, Heinemann Library

The Life and Work of Paul Klee, Sean Connolly, Heinemann Library

More paintings by Wassily Kandinsky to see

Cossacks, Tate Modern, London

Composition IX, Museum of Modern Art, Paris

a b c d e f g h i j k l m n o p q r s t u v w x y z

Index